V

BEFORE YOU START YOUR DAY

A 21-Day Leadership Devotional

VANCE K. JACKSON, JR.

Before You Start Your Day: A 21-Day Leadership Devotional
ISBN: 978-1-7369832-2-5
Published by 5th Gen Publishing, LLC.
© 2021 Vance K. Jackson, Jr.
www.VanceKJackson.com

Printed in the United States of America. All rights reserved. No portion of this book may be reproduced, stored in a retrieval system, or transmitted in any form or by any means—electronic, mechanical, photocopy, recording, scanning, or other—except for brief quotations in critical reviews or articles, without the prior written permission of the publisher.

Scripture quotations taken from the Amplified® Bible (AMPC), Copyright © 1954, 1958, 1962, 1964, 1965, 1987 by The Lockman Foundation Used by permission. www.lockman.org

Scripture quotations from The Authorized King James Version (KJV). Rights in the Authorized Version in the United Kingdom are vested in the Crown. Reproduced by permission of the Crown's patentee, Cambridge University Press.

Scripture quotations marked (MSG) are taken from THE MESSAGE, copyright © 1993, 2002, 2018 by Eugene H. Peterson. Used by permission of NavPress, represented by Tyndale House Publishers. All rights reserved.

Scripture quotations marked (NIV) are taken from the Holy Bible, New International Version®, NIV®. Copyright © 1973, 1978, 1984, 2011 by Biblica, Inc.™ Used by permission of Zondervan. All rights reserved worldwide. www.zondervan.com The "NIV" and "New International Version" are trademarks registered in the United States Patent and Trademark Office by Biblica, Inc.™

Scripture quotations marked (NLT) are taken from the Holy Bible, New Living Translation, copyright © 1996, 2004, 2015 by Tyndale House Foundation. Used by permission of Tyndale House Publishers, Inc., Carol Stream, Illinois 60188. All rights reserved.

Library of Congress Cataloging-in-Publication Data

Library of Congress Control Number: 2021912970

But God hath chosen the foolish things of the world to confound the wise; and God hath chosen the weak things of the world to confound the things which are mighty

1 CORINTHIANS 1:27 KJV

TABLE OF CONTENTS

DAY 1
With Every Breath 11

DAY 2
Seek Me First 15

DAY 3
Patience is Powerful..............................21

DAY 4
Seek Me Early...................................25

DAY 5
Treasure His Word 29

DAY 6
To Everything there is a Season 33

DAY 7
There is No New Thing Under the Sun.............37

DAY 8
Spirit of Fear 41

DAY 9
Launch Out into the Deep 45

DAY 10
Go to the Ant 49

DAY 11
Arise Out of Your Sleep 53

DAY 12
The Thoughts of the Diligent 57

DAY 13
The Hand of the Diligent 61

DAY 14
The Slothful Does Not Roast 65

DAY 15
The Soul of the Sluggard. 69

DAY 16
Seest Thou a Man Diligent in His Business?. 73

DAY 17
Know the State of Thy Flocks 77

DAY 18
Before You Build. 81

DAY 19
Don't Look Back. 85

DAY 20
Harden Not Your Heart 89

DAY 21
Keep Your Heart with All Diligence. 93

Day 1

WITH EVERY BREATH

Let every thing that hath breath praise the Lord.
Praise ye the Lord.

PSALMS 150:6 KJV

Today, as you are reading these words, God has blessed you with a precious gift—"The Gift of Life." Psalm 150:6 KJV declares, "Let every thing that hath breath praise the Lord. Praise ye the Lord." The Amplified Version expounds on Psalm 150:6 AMPC in the following manner, "Let everything that have breath and every breath of life praise the Lord! Praise the Lord! (Hallelujah!)"

Let every breath of your life praise the Lord. Before you start your day, choose to praise the Lord. Let every breath that you breathe praise the Lord. Let every aspect of your life praise the Lord. Let everything that you both say and do praise the Lord. Choose to start your day by praising the Lord. Initiate your day with thanksgiving. With every breath, choose to praise the Lord.

According to Strong's Concordance, the Hebrew word for "praise", is "halal" (H1984), which means, "To shine, to shine of God's favor, to flash forth light, boast, to be boastful, to be made praiseworthy, to be commended, be worthy of praise, glory, to make one's boast, to make a fool of, make into a fool."

Let every aspect of your life 'halal' God. Let every part of your life praise God. Let every aspect of your life shine and give God glory. If there's an aspect of your life that's not "shining" or reflecting the Glory of God, choose to surrender it to the Lord. Let every aspect of your life radiate and reflect the light of Christ both in private and in public.

Let every aspect of your life reflect the favor of God. Let every aspect of your life boast in the Lord. Let every aspect of your life be praiseworthy of honor and glory. Let every part of your life make a boast of the Lord and make a fool of the enemy.

Psalm 115:17 KJV declares, "The dead praise not the Lord, neither any that go down into silence." The dead cannot 'halal' the Lord. The dead cannot praise the Lord. The dead cannot give glory to God. The dead cannot shine of God's favor. Dead things and dead dreams cannot 'halal' the Lord. The dead cannot exalt Him. Give every dead thing over to God. I pray that God ministers to and revives your old, forgotten and abandoned dreams. I pray that God gives you the strength to pick up your purpose again. I pray that God gives you the courage to dream again.

As you read these words, I pray that God ministers to every area of your heart. I pray that you hear His Voice through the wisdom, insight, and revelation contained on these pages. I pray that God reveals His Word, Wisdom, Insight, and Revelation to you in a new, fresh, and relevant way. I pray that you hear His Voice in between each line.

I pray that God opens up and increases your insight, wisdom, and understanding as you read each page. I pray that God multiplies your wisdom, insight, understanding, and revelation as you engage His Heart. Each day, I pray that you diligently crave more of Him. It is my earnest desire and my hope that as you diligently deploy and apply His Principles and Precepts, that His Word comes alive within the walls of your heart and life.

It is my desire that you honor, exalt, and 'halal' God with every breath that you breathe. Choose to honor Christ within the walls of your home. Choose to honor God within the walls of your life. Choose to cherish and treasure every Principle and Precept of Christ deep within the infrastructure of your heart.

PRAYER

Father God, in the Name of Jesus, I thank You for my life. Father, I thank You for every breath that I breathe.

Father, I thank You that You're giving me revelation and insight regarding Your Purpose for my life. Lord, You are good, and my heart surrenders to You.

Father, You are good, and Your Mercy is Everlasting. Father, my heart will forever praise You. Father, my heart will forever exalt You. Father, my heart will forever 'halal' You. Lord, I will forever bow to You.

Father, let Your Word saturate the ground of my heart. Father, water the ground of my heart with Your Word. Father, let Your Peace cover every area of my life. Lord, let Your Peace cover every area of my home. Father, let Your Joy fill my heart.

Lord, remove anything within the walls of my heart that is not like You. Father, let my heart reflect Your Love and Character. Father, I turn to You, and I will forever serve You.

In Jesus' Name. Amen.

Day 2

SEEK ME FIRST

But seek ye first the kingdom of God, and his righteousness; and all these things shall be added unto you.

MATTHEW 6:33 KJV

Choose to seek Christ. Start your day with the intention to seek His Way of doing things. Seek His Way of doing things in every area of your life. Choose to settle and posture your heart to seek Christ.

Deuteronomy 30:15 KJV declares, "See, I have set before thee this day life and good, and death and evil;" God has 'gifted' you with the ability to choose. God has 'gifted' you with the opportunity to steward your day, so choose to submit your agenda over to Him. Surrender your processes and thoughts over to Him. Surrender your ways to Him.

Choose to seek Christ in every aspect of your life. Let His Way become your life's blueprint. Choose to serve Him in every aspect of your life. Choose to submit and surrender every area of your heart over to Christ. Matthew 6:33 NLT declares, "Seek the Kingdom of God above all else, and live righteously, and he will give you everything you need."

Above all else, seek Christ first. Let His Way become your priority. Let His Way shape the framework of your character. Let His Way mature the foundation of your integrity. In all things, seek Christ first. Seek Him first and live righteously.

Seek God in both spiritual and natural things. Seek Him first in matters of the heart. Seek Him in handling your business affairs. Seek Him in handling family matters. Seek Him in your financial affairs. Seek Him in all things and He will give you everything that you need.

If you have an Earthly need, know that your Heavenly Father is a good Father and will give you what you need. In fact, He will give you more than what you need. The Amplified Version (AMPC) expounds upon John 10:10 AMPC in the following manner, "The thief comes only in order to steal and kill and destroy. I came that they may have and enjoy life, and have it in abundance (to the full, till it overflows)."

Jesus came so that you may have and enjoy life, and have it in abundance (to the full, till it overflows). Know that God cares about you. He cares about your needs. He cares about every aspect of your life.

Choose not to be like the world, know that God knows what you are in need of before you ask. Matthew 6:8 KJV declares, "Be not ye therefore like unto them: for your Father knoweth what things ye have need of, before ye ask him." Do you not know that He will take care of your needs?

God, your Heavenly Father, wants you to seek Him in all that you do. If you choose to seek Him first, then all these 'other' things will be added unto you. Choose not to let your heart crave and worship the things of this world.

Exodus 20:3 KJV declares, "Thou shalt have no other gods before me." Exodus 20:3 New Living Translation (NLT) puts it this way, "You must not have any other god but me." What is your heart craving? What is your heart's appetite? Are you craving the things of this world or are you craving the things of God? Behind every ungodly desire, your heart is secretly feeding a hidden idol. Behind every perverted and ungodly craving, there is an idol that your heart is secretly worshipping.

Galatians 5:1 KJV declares, "Stand fast therefore in the liberty wherewith Christ hath made us free, and be not entangled again with the yoke of bondage." Choose to set your heart on the Principles and Precepts of God. Let His Word sink deep into the rich soil of your heart. Let your heart crave Him. Let your heart honor Him. Let your heart 'halal' Him. Choose to seek Christ first.

What does your heart crave? What does your heart desire? Who does your heart crave? Who does your heart long for? What are you seeking? Are you seeking Christ or are you seeking to serve and worship the things of this world? Are you amplifying the things of this world over honoring Christ? What are you elevating within the borders of your heart? Who are you exalting?

Are you seeking to acquire 'stuff' more than you are seeking the Heart of God? Are you seeking that promotion more than you're seeking to surrender to God? Are you seeking the approval of people more than you are seeking the approval of God? Are you seeking the opinion of man more than the 'Yes' from God? Are you seeking influence, status, position, popularity, and authority more than the approval of God? Choose to seek God first. Let His Way lead your day and shape your character. In all things seek Him.

Seek His Counsel. Seek His Insight. Seek His Wisdom. Seek His Understanding. Let His Word shape the framework of your heart. Let His Word shape the framework of your day.

Let His Word shape the framework of your decisions. Let His Way shape the framework of your life.

Let God lead your day. Seek Him first. Before you grab that first cup of coffee or your favorite drink, choose to seek Him. Let Christ start your day. Before you take care of your normal daily obligations choose to seek Him first. Let Christ establish the blueprint of your day.

Let Christ lead and soften your heart. Let His Word wash and reset your heart. Maybe you're about to handle a major business matter at work. Choose to seek the Character and Heart of God in the affairs of your business. Choose to seek Him before you respond. Choose to seek Him before you execute. Choose to seek His Way of doing things.

Choose to seek Christ in all that you say and do. Seek Christ even in how you handle your conduct, both in private and in public. Seek Him on how to lead, manage, and rule the affairs of your day. Seek Christ on how to rule the affairs of your business.

Like Solomon, seek Him on how to handle matters justly. Seek God on how to lead and serve those who submit to you. Seek God on how to execute justly. Seek God on how to execute with wisdom. Seek God on how to lead your family. Seek God on how to handle the hearts of those whom you steward. Seek God on how to handle the "Heart Affairs" of those whom God has assigned to you.

Whether you're a husband, or a wife; a mom or a dad; a board member, a manager or CEO, your position and place of authority is granted to you by God and you are to steward and govern your place of authority well. Romans 13:1 KJV declares, "Let every soul be subject unto the higher powers. For there is no power but of God: the powers that be are ordained of God." The New Living Translation expounds upon Romans 13:1 NLT in the following manner, "Everyone must submit to governing authorities. For all authority comes from God, and those in positions of authority have been placed there by God."

All authority comes from God. Whether you're in management, a husband, a parent, a Board member, an executive, mayor, governor, senator, politician or an overseer;—all authority comes from God. Authority is a gift from God. Seek Him on how to steward your platform. Seek Christ on how to steward your position. Seek Him on how to steward your day well. Steward your season. Steward your time. Steward your moment.

PRAYER

Father God, in the Name of Jesus, I choose to seek You with all of my heart. Father, I choose to submit to You. Father, I surrender every area of my life over to You.

Father God, in the Name of Jesus, I fully surrender to Your Way of doing things. Father, I choose to surrender to You and I choose to seek Your Wise Counsel. Father, I seek Your Wisdom and Your Way.

Father, open up my understanding and let me hear Your Voice clearly. I glean to You for instruction and insight. Lord, let Your Word shape my character. Let Your Word lead my day.

Father, I surrender to You. I cast down every idol and submit to You. I bow down before You and cast down my crown before Your Throne. Lord, lead me. Father, guide me. Lord, You are the Savior of my heart.

In Jesus' Name. Amen.

Day 3

PATIENCE IS POWERFUL

He that is slow to anger is better than the mighty; and he that ruleth his spirit than he that taketh a city.

PROVERBS 16:32 KJV

Let patience lead your day. Let patience cultivate the ground of your heart. Let patience rule your character. Let patience set the tone of your day. Let patience cultivate the ground of your day. Let patience cultivate and shape the framework of your decisions. Let patience lead you. You choose. Rule your spirit or let the cares and waves of the world rule your response. Let His Word rule your world.

Proverbs 16:32 KJV declares, "He that is slow to anger is better than the mighty; and he that ruleth his spirit than he that taketh a city." The New Living Translation expounds on Proverbs 16:32 NLT in the following manner, "Better to be patient than powerful; better to have self-control than to conquer a city."

It's better to be patient than to be powerful. In fact, patience is power. Whether you're leading in business, leading in government, leading in the community, leading your family, leading in ministry, leading, or serving behind the scenes, or in front of the camera, patience is needed.

No matter your role, no matter your position, patience is needed. In fact, executives need patience in order to effectively make good, sober, and sound decisions. Executives, and those in authority, need patience as they collect information, data, and insight from various sources and trusted advisors. Those in authority need patience in order to implement just policies that benefit all.

In addition to governing well, executives in business need patience in order to steward and effectively manage the business affairs of their firm. Executives in government need patience in order to effectively manage the resources under their stewardship. Even executives of the home need patience in order to steward the daily affairs of their family. Patience is needed in every aspect of your life.

In fact, according to James 1:19 KJV, those who deploy and practice patience tend to lead and govern well. James 1:19 KJV declares, "Wherefore, my beloved brethren, let every man be swift to hear, slow to speak, slow to wrath:" Mature executives are practitioners of patience. They are 'Swift to hear and slow to speak'. Executives are students of patience and faithfully study and deploy its principles and precepts in their daily practice.

Proverbs 17:28 KJV declares even fools who practice patience 'appear' to be wise, "Even a fool, when he holdeth his peace, is counted wise: and he that shutteth his lips is esteemed a man of understanding." The New International Version expounds on Proverbs 17:28 NIV in the following manner, "Even fools are thought wise if they keep silent, and discerning if they hold their tongues."

Choose to deploy the art of patience in every area of your life. Deploy the skill of patience in business. Deploy patience in your everyday conduct. Deploy the strategic tool of patience even in challenging times. The art of patience will help you in difficult times. The art of patience will guide you through tumultuous times.

Maybe, you are in need of patience. Hebrews 10:36 KJV declares, "For ye have need of patience, that, after ye have done the will of God, ye might receive the promise." Through the lens and framework of patience—patience will lead you to the Promise. Patience will guard and guide your emotions. Put patience into practice and watch your response to difficult and challenging matters transform.

Patience produces a mature response. In fact, patience sharpens your executive emotional intelligence. Leaders in the Bible used the tool of patience before conquering new territories. Kings of the Bible deployed patience before executing upon a task or project.

Luke 14:28 NLT declares, "But don't begin until you count the cost. For who would begin construction of a building without first calculating the cost to see if there is enough money to finish it?" Before you begin a task, project, or assignment, deploy patience. Before you begin a large project, patiently count the cost.

Patience is a gift. Patience is a skill. Patience can be cultivated. Patience can be developed. Patience can be matured and sharpened within the 'heart framework' of all leaders. Practice patience and you'll grow as a leader. Practice patience and watch those under your stewardship grow and develop as leaders.

Psalm 103:8 KJV declares, "The Lord is merciful and gracious, slow to anger, and plenteous in mercy." Even Jesus Christ, the "Ultimate Leader," deployed patience. The Lord is gracious and is slow to anger. The Lord is Patient. The Lord is Just. The Lord is Merciful. The Lord is Kind. Choose to reflect the Character of Christ and practice patience.

Practice patience before you abruptly respond. Patience is a leadership trait and requires discipline and intentionality. Patience is a choice, and mature leaders deploy this disciplined skill in order to rule wisely.

How can you effectively lead others if you don't have the discipline to lead and control your response? How can you effectively govern others if you can't govern your emotions? Practice patience and you'll lead the mighty. Deploy patience and you'll rule the strong. Make the practice of patience your priority.

PRAYER

Father God, in the Name of Jesus, I thank You for shaping the Character of my heart. Father, I thank You for leading every aspect of my life. Father, I choose to serve and honor You. Father, I choose to seek You with all of my heart.

Father, I thank You for patience. Father, let patience guide me. Father, let patience shape the framework of my character. Father, I thank You for guiding my heart. Father, I thank You for guiding my soul.

Lord, lead me. Lord, guide my path. Father, lead and regulate my emotions. Father, guide my house through tumultuous times. Lord, lead my response in difficult circumstances.

Lord, strengthen my character. Father, lead my actions in private and in public. Let patience rule the framework of my life. Father, light my path.

Let Your Favor surround me. Let Your Peace shield me. Let Your Mercy cover me. Father, I choose to surrender to You. Lord, lead my response and guide my footsteps. Father, I am Yours forever.

In Jesus' Name. Amen.

Day 4

SEEK ME EARLY

I love them that love me; and those that seek me early shall find me.

PROVERBS 8:17 KJV

Proverbs 8:12 AMPC declares, "I, Wisdom [from God], make prudence my dwelling, and I find out knowledge and discretion." Before you start your day, choose to seek wisdom from the Heart of God.

Let wisdom dwell richly within every area of your heart. Let wisdom dwell richly within every area of your life. Let wisdom shape the framework of your heart. Let the fabric of wisdom shape the decisions that you make. Proverbs 8:17 NLT declares, "...those that seek me early shall find me." Choose to search out wisdom.

Choose to crave wisdom. Choose to seek the Wisdom of God for every circumstance of your life. Let the Wisdom of God govern your day. In fact, Proverbs 8:17 KJV declares, "...those that seek me early shall find me." Choose to seek out wisdom early.

Seek the Wisdom of God early in the situation. Seek His Counsel early in the circumstance. Those who seek out the Wisdom of God will find Him. Matthew 5:6 KJV declares, Blessed are they which do hunger and thirst after righteousness: for they shall be filled." His Word is His Wisdom.

Those who hunger after God's Word shall be filled. Those who crave God's Way of doing things shall be satisfied. Seek Him early in the circumstance. Seek Him early and He shall fill you. Seek His Insight and Counsel and you shall be filled.

James 1:5 KJV declares, "If any of you lack wisdom, let him ask of God, that giveth to all men liberally, and upbraideth not; and it shall be given him." If you lack wisdom simply ask God and He will give you wisdom freely from His Heart. God lavishly gives wisdom to those who ask, just ask.

The New International Version (NIV) expounds on James 1:5 NIV in the following manner, "If any of you lacks wisdom, you should ask God, who gives generously to all without finding fault, and it will be given to you." Just ask your Heavenly Father for wisdom. The mistakes, shortcomings, and shortfalls of your past doesn't matter. Ask God for the wisdom on how to handle your day.

Before you start your day, ask God for wisdom on how to handle the affairs of your day. Ask God for wisdom on how to engage with and handle the heart of your family. Ask God for wisdom on how to engage with coworkers, peers, and colleagues. If you're married, ask God for wisdom on how to handle the heart of your spouse. If you're engaged, ask God for wisdom on how to handle the heart of your fiancé. Ask God for wisdom in all matters of life.

Ask God for wisdom regarding big and small things. Ask God for wisdom on how to solve problems in the marketplace. Ask God for wisdom on how to innovate in business. Ask God for wisdom and creative ideas on how to innovate in your daily affairs.

Proverbs 8:12 KJV declares, "I wisdom dwell with prudence, and find out knowledge of witty inventions." Witty inventions are married to wisdom. Witty processes are birthed out of wisdom. Witty strategies are tied to wisdom. Ask God to give you witty and innovative ideas. Ask God to give you answers to challenging problems. Ask God to pour witty ideas into your heart.

1 Corinthians 2:9 KJV declares, "But as it is written, Eye hath not seen, nor ear heard, neither have entered into the heart of man, the things which God hath prepared for them that love him." May God give you wisdom that eyes have not seen. May God pour witty answers in your mouth that ears have not heard. May He give you creative solutions that have not entered into the heart of man. May God give you the grace to answer challenging problems. May God give you the grace to be the solution to the "King's Problem."

May you be known for creating solutions. May you have the reputation for being a "Problem Solver." May you be set apart from amongst your peers. May your efforts and work ethic be revered. May you be known as uncommon and full of character.

Daniel 1:20 KJV declares, "And in all matters of wisdom and understanding, that the king enquired of them, he found them ten times better than all the magicians and astrologers that were in all his realm." Daniel and his team were ten times better than their peers. Ask God to give you wisdom, insight, and counsel that is ten times better than the world.

Daniel and his colleagues outperformed their counterparts. God gave Daniel and his colleagues incomparable wisdom. God gave Daniel and his colleagues the wisdom to innovate and to solve challenging problems. Who's on your team? Who are you associated with? Ask God to surround you with those who are filled with wisdom. Ask God to surround you with "Wisdom Carriers."

Proverbs 11:14 KJV declares, "Where no counsel is, the people fall: but in the multitude of counsellors there is safety." Proverbs 11:14 AMPC puts it this way, "Where no wise guidance is, the people fall, but in the multitude of counselors there is safety." Ask God to surround you with wise Counselors. Choose to seek God's Counsel. Choose to seek His Wisdom and God will set you apart.

PRAYER

Father God, in the Name of Jesus, I will seek You early. Father, my heart will seek You early. Father, I will seek Your Face before the storm forms. Father, I choose to seek Your Wisdom, Guidance, and Insight.

Father, lead me. Father, guide me. Father, I will forever seek Your Way of doing things. Father, my heart trusts in You. Lord, my heart honors You. Father, You are my King and I will forever serve You.

Father, You are my very present help. Father, lead my path. Lord, order my steps. Father, like Daniel, grant me the wisdom to execute in excellence. Father, grace me to execute ten times better than the world.

Father, I choose to surround myself with wise, Godly, and mature counselors. Father, anoint my hands to do Your work. Father, anoint my heart to do Your Will. Father, anoint my mind to do things Your Way. Father, I honor You and choose to surrender my heart to You forever.

In Jesus' Name. Amen.

Day 5

TREASURE HIS WORD

*Thy word have I hid in mine heart,
that I might not sin against thee.*

PSALMS 119:11 KJV

As you choose to plan out your day, choose to hide His Word within the walls of your heart. According to Strong's Concordance, the Hebrew word for, "hide" used in Psalm 119:11 KJV, is "tsaphan" (H6845) which means, 'To hide, treasure, or store up'.

Choose to hide, store up, and treasure God's Word within the walls of your heart. Choose to highly value His Word deep within every area of your heart. Let His Word shape the framework of your day. As you go about making daily decisions, choose to let His Word lead your response. Choose to hide His Word deep within the walls of your heart.

Before you start your day, choose to meditate on and digest His Word. Choose to let His Word guide how you lead others. Choose to let His Word guide how you serve others. Choose to build your family and your life on the Principles and Precepts of His Word. Be intentional and diligently set your heart on His Word.

Psalm 119:11 suggests, when you hide or 'store up' on His Word, you're nourishing the soil of your heart with His Principles and Precepts. Matthew 4:4 KJV puts it this way, "It is written, Man shall not live by bread alone, but by every word that proceedeth out of the mouth of God." Choose to continually feed your heart with God's Word. Nourish the ground of your heart with the Word of God.

Let His Wisdom cover the ground of your heart. Let His Word run deep within the deep-seated root system of your heart. Let His Word speak louder than the waves of the world. Let His Word ring louder in your ears than the opinions of man.

Let His Word conquer every fear within the walls of your heart. Let His Word triumph over every doubt. Choose to meditate and dwell upon His Word daily. Joshua 1:8 KJV puts it this way, "This book of the law shall not depart out of thy mouth; but thou shalt meditate therein day and night, that thou mayest observe to do according to all that is written therein: for then thou shalt make thy way prosperous, and then thou shalt have good success."

Treasure His Word and you will have good success. Let His Word lead your house. Let His Word guide your ship. Let His Word break up every stubborn and hardened area of your heart. "For thus saith the Lord to the men of Judah and Jerusalem, Break up your fallow ground, and sow not among thorns." Jeremiah 4:3 KJV.

PRAYER

Father God, in the Name of Jesus, I choose to treasure Your Word. Father, I choose to store up Your Word within the ground of my heart. Father, I choose to serve and honor You in private and in public.

Father, I choose to be nourished by every Word that proceeds out of Your mouth. I choose to lay down my crown and surrender to Your Way of doing things. Father, I choose to lay down my cares and submit to You. Father, I choose to lay down my talents, skills, and abilities and surrender to You.

Father, I choose to surrender to You. Father, I choose to seek Your Counsel in every area of my life. Father, I ask that You remove the blinders from my eyes so that I see Your Word more clearly. Father, I ask that You open up my ears to hear Your Voice clearly. Father, lead my heart. Lord, lead my day.

In Jesus' Name. Amen.

Day 6

TO EVERYTHING THERE IS A SEASON

*To every thing there is a season,
and a time to every purpose under the heaven.*

ECCLESIASTES 3:1 KJV

To everything there is a season. Choose to execute in season. God has a timing for everything; His timing is perfect. His timing has purpose. His timing carries weight. In fact, according to Strong's Concordance, the Hebrew word for, 'season' is, 'zeman' (H2165) which means, "Set time, appointed time, time."

Choose to execute in season. Choose to execute in your set time. Choose to execute when God says move. When God commands you to launch, it's time to launch. Move in God's appointed time. Do what God has called you to do. God's timing is perfect.

Procrastination is a trick of the enemy. Procrastination is a tool that the enemy uses, to distract you from fulfilling your assignment. Procrastination is a strategic weapon that the enemy deploys in order to slow you down and to even discourage you from fulfilling your destiny. In fact, procrastination is a form of slack, sloth, and pride.

Choose to execute upon the things that you're able to control today. If it's in your power to do it today, don't delay—execute. Proverbs 18:9 KJV declares, "He also that is slothful in his work is brother to him that is a great waster." Sloth is one of the many spirits behind procrastination.

He that is slothful wastes time. He that is slothful wastes resources. He that is slothful rarely completes assignments. Slothful people are sporadic in execution. In fact, according to James 1:8 KJV, "A double minded man is unstable in all his ways." Slothful people are double-minded. The slothful are unstable and are not consistent.

Choose to eliminate sloth in every area of your life. Choose not to be double minded. Choose to be diligent. The double-minded are unstable and unreliable. Choose to be reliable, consistent, and dependable. Now is the season to execute. Choose not to put off a task for tomorrow and do what's in your control today.

Visions are delayed when you procrastinate. Dreams are forfeited when you procrastinate. In fact, procrastination is delayed obedience. Stagnation is the fruit of procrastination. Procrastination stunts your growth. Procrastination paralyzes your destiny.

Choose to execute and divorce yourself from waiting for the perfect time. Waiting for the perfect time is an excuse that delays destiny. Choose to seek God and execute in His timing. Execute when He leads you. Execute when He commands you to "Come out on the water." Execute when He commands you to "Launch out into the deep." Execute when He tells you to 'Go.'

Don't let fear tie you to stagnation. Don't let fear imprison your destiny. Don't let fear hijack your purpose. Don't waste your breath with excuses. Today, you've been given a gift—the gift of life. Choose to execute and let the work of your hands speak for itself. Let the work of your hands glorify God.

Don't let excuses fill your lips. Divorce yourself from making excuses. Divorce yourself from procrastination. Divorce yourself from the spirit of fear. Choose to launch. Choose to execute. Choose to write that book today. Choose to build that business today. Choose to make the decision to go back to school today. Choose to move today. God has given you the gift of 'today.'

Choose to obey God today and move forward in season—His Season. To everything there is a purpose. God has a purpose for this season. Do not despise your season. Do not despise your moment. Surrender and submit to God's timing. His timing is perfect. His timing is just. His timing has purpose.

PRAYER

Father God, in the Name of Jesus, I choose to submit to Your Way of doing things. Father, I choose to let go of procrastination. Father, I choose to execute as I hear Your Voice. Father, I choose to submit to Your timing. Father, Your timing has purpose. Father, Your timing has significance.

Lord, I choose to trust You with all of my heart. Father, I refuse to surrender to fear. In the Name of Jesus, I choose to divorce myself from fear. Fear does not have dominion over my heart. Fear will not rule me. Fear has no place in the walls of my heart. Father, I choose to serve You forever.

In Jesus' Name. Amen.

Day 7

THERE IS NO NEW THING UNDER THE SUN

The thing that hath been, it is that which shall be; and that which is done is that which shall be done: and there is no new thing under the sun.

ECCLESIASTES 1:9 KJV

There's no need to "reinvent" the wheel. Ecclesiastes 1:9 KJV declares that there is no new thing under the sun. Every process, every protocol, every procedure comes from God. Innovation comes from God. Witty ideas and inventions come from God. Wisdom comes from Him. Ingenuity comes from Him. He holds all things in His Hands. Nothing is new to God. He is the Author and Creator of all things.

Hebrews 11:3 AMPC declares, "By faith we understand that the worlds [during the successive ages] were framed (fashioned, put in order, and equipped for their intended purpose) by the word of God, so that what we see was not made out of things which are visible." Every age of the world was authored by God Himself. So before you start your day, why not surrender your day to the One who authored eternity.

Before you start your day, why not ask the one who already occupies the future. Before you start your day, choose to seek the

Author of time itself. There is nothing new under the sun. God is the One who commanded the sun to rise in the morning and to set in the evening. He authored the path of every molecule that exists. He set the laws of physics in place. He even numbered the hairs on your head.

Job 38:4-11 KJV declares, "Where wast thou when I laid the foundations of the earth? declare, if thou hast understanding. Who hath laid the measures thereof, if thou knowest? or who hath stretched the line upon it? Whereupon are the foundations thereof fastened? or who laid the corner stone thereof; When the morning stars sang together, and all the sons of God shouted for joy? Or who shut up the sea with doors, when it brake forth, as if it had issued out of the womb? When I made the cloud the garment thereof, and thick darkness a swaddlingband for it, And brake up for it my decreed place, and set bars and doors, And said, Hitherto shalt thou come, but no further: and here shall thy proud waves be stayed?"

God laid the foundations of the Earth. He created Heaven and the Earth. He told the waves to proceed no further. The host of Heaven bows to Him. According to Revelation 19:16 KJV He is Lord of lords. Every lord, all authority, every power, from every age bows to Him. He is King of all kings.

Proverbs 21:1 KJV declares, "The king's heart is in the hand of the Lord, as the rivers of water: he turneth it whithersoever he will." The heart of the king is in His Hands. God turns the hearts of kings in your favor. God turns and controls the heart of kings. He controls the heart of those who are in authority and He can turn it in your favor.

The heart of those who are in authority are in His Hands. The heart of the "Decision Maker" is in His Hands. The heart of your manager is in His Hands. The heart of the judge is in

His Hands. Seek the Heart of God and let His Hand turn the hearts of kings.

Revelation 1:8 KJV declares, "I am Alpha and Omega, the beginning and the ending, saith the Lord, which is, and which was, and which is to come, the Almighty." He is Alpha and Omega. He is the Beginning and the End. There's nothing new that He has not seen. Before time began—He was. And when time ends—He shall be.

Revelation 21:23 KJV declares, "And the city had no need of the sun, neither of the moon, to shine in it: for the glory of God did lighten it, and the Lamb is the light thereof." His Glory is so magnificent and brilliant that His Glory outshines the sun. His Presence outshines His creation. Nothing can "outmaneuver" Him. There is no process that can "outthink" Him. There is no procedure that can "outrank" Him. Nothing can "outshine" Him. God has the final say. His Authority is sovereign. His Authority is everlasting. His Authority has no end.

So, before your day begins, before this moment in time begins, seek the Counsel of the One who has no end. His Glory is all sufficient. His timing is all encapsulating. Nothing is new to Him. Nothing catches God off guard. Just because it's new to you does not mean that it's new to God.

God saw the storm form before time began. There is no problem that He cannot handle. There is no problem that He cannot solve. He is God Almighty and He cares for you. Go to the One who has never lost a battle. Go to the One who is incapable of being defeated. Go to the One whose garments are soaked in the blood of His enemies.

Revelation 19:13 KJV declares, "And he was clothed with a vesture dipped in blood: and his name is called The Word of God." Go to the One who stands as Victor even at the end of time. Your day is but a microcosm when compared to eternity, and eternity is in God's Hands. This moment is like a grain of sand on the seashore. But God loves you so much that He even cares about your day.

Psalm 90:12 NIV declares, "Teach us to number our days, that we may gain a heart of wisdom." Let God lead your heart. Let God lead your day. Let God give you the wisdom to steward this moment. Let God give you wisdom to steward this day well.

There is nothing new under the sun. There is nothing new to Him; not even your day. This day may be new to you, but it's not new to God. He is Omnipresent and He occupies all of space and time. Surrender your day to the One who saw this day before time began.

PRAYER

Father God, in the Name of Jesus, I thank You for life. Lord, I thank You that You hold all of time in Your Hands. Father, You are Sovereign and there is no one like You.

Lord, You are the Giver of life. Lord, You are the Giver of wisdom. According to James 1:5, You give wisdom to those who ask. Father, I ask You for wisdom.

Father, I ask You for wisdom to navigate my day. Father, I ask You for wisdom to navigate challenging circumstances. Father, I ask You for wisdom to overcome headwinds and obstacles.

Father, I ask You for wisdom to navigate my financial affairs. Father, I ask You for wisdom to lead my family. Lord, I ask You for wisdom to navigate the emotions of my heart. Lord, I ask You for wisdom to lead my day.

In Jesus' Name. Amen.

Day 8

SPIRIT OF FEAR

For God hath not given us the spirit of fear; but of power, and of love, and of a sound mind.

2 TIMOTHY 1:7 KJV

According to Strong's Concordance, the Greek word for, 'fear' is, 'deilia' (G1167) which means, "Timidity, fearfulness, cowardice." Choose not to start your day with fear and timidity. God has not given you the spirit of fear, but of power.

According to Strong's Concordance, the Greek word for, 'power' is, 'dynamis' (G1411) which means, "Strength, power, ability, moral power and excellence of soul, the power and influence which belong to riches and wealth."

God has not given you the spirit of a coward, He has given you the strength, power, and ability to tackle your day with wisdom. Choose to conquer your day. God has given you the ability and moral power to stand up in times of adversity. He has given you the power to lead justly.

God has not given you the spirit to draw back. God has not called you to be timid, He has given you the power to rule justly in the face of your enemies.

Jeremiah 1:8 KJV declares, "Be not afraid of their faces: for I am with thee to deliver thee, saith the Lord." The Lord is with you. Don't be afraid of their opinions, the Lord is with you. Don't be afraid of their power and influence, the Lord is with you. Don't be afraid of their political influence, the Lord is with you.

Don't be afraid of what they think or say about you, the Lord is with you. God has not given you the spirit of fear, but of bold confidence. Don't be afraid of their hidden agenda, the Lord is with you.

Don't be afraid of the snares and traps set by the enemy, for the Lord is with you. Luke 10:19 KJV declares, "Behold, I give unto you power to tread on serpents and scorpions, and over all the power of the enemy: and nothing shall by any means hurt you."

According to Strong's Concordance, the Greek word for, 'Power' used in Luke 10:19 KJV is, 'exousia' (G1849) which means, "Power of choice, liberty of doing as one pleases, leave or permission, physical and mental power, the ability or strength with which one is endued, which he either possesses or exercises, the power of authority (influence) and of right (privilege)."

God has given you the power to choose. You have the choice to tread on serpents in every area of your life. You have the power to overcome the enemy in every area of your life. God has given you the mental fortitude and the physical strength to overcome the enemy in every area of your life. God has given you the mental tenacity to overcome and conquer every stronghold of the enemy. God has given you the power to overcome and overthrow all the power of the enemy.

Interestingly, the word, 'Power' was used twice in Luke 10:19 KJV. According to Strong's Concordance, the Greek word for, 'Power' used in the second part of Luke 10:19 KJV is, 'dynamis' (G1411) which means, "Power for performing miracles, strength, power, and ability." God has given you the strength and the power to overcome and resist the tactics and strategies of the enemy.

James 4:7 KJV declares, "Submit yourselves therefore to God. Resist the devil, and he will flee from you." According to Strong's Concordance, the Greek word for, 'Resist' is, 'anthistēmi' (G436) which means, "To set one's self against, to withstand, to oppose." Before you start your day, set yourself against the enemy. God has given you the mental fortitude to resist the enemy. Set your mind on Christ. Set your mind on Christ's Way of doing things.

Fear is one of the enemy's weapons that incite panic, worry, and doubt. The weapon of fear wants to paralyze and stunt your destiny. The enemy is after your mind. Christ came to give you a sound mind. Christ came to settle your heart and to give you peace. Choose to exercise faith. Choose to dismantle the weapon of fear by executing in faith. For God has not given you the spirit of fear; but of power, and of love, and of a sound mind.

Ephesians 6:16 KJV declares, "Above all, taking the shield of faith, wherewith ye shall be able to quench all the fiery darts of the wicked." God has given you the faith to quench all of the fiery darts of the enemy. Choose to live courageously. Choose not to be timid. Choose to actively resist the devil throughout the day and he will flee. Fear has no place in your life. Fear has no place in your day.

Deuteronomy 28:7 KJV declares, "The Lord shall cause thine enemies that rise up against thee to be smitten before thy face: they shall come out against thee one way, and flee before thee seven ways." Let fear flee seven ways before you. Choose to use the Word of God to disarm the grip of fear from off of your heart. Choose to fearlessly start your day.

Don't allow fear to creep in the borders of your mind. When fear tries to creep in the borders of your mind, choose to meditate on His Word. For God did not put the spirit of fear in you, God created you to tread upon the enemy. God created you to live in and walk by faith and to crush the enemy's kingdom of fear.

Where fear dwells, faith shrinks. Fear will cause you to forfeit your destiny. When fear tries to raise its head, choose to crush it at all cost. Don't allow the seed of fear to plant itself in any area of your life. Choose to execute upon that vision that God has given you. Don't let the voice of fear speak louder than what God has declared over your life. Choose to crush fear and seek Christ's Way of doing things.

Remember, where fear dwells, stagnation is nearby. In the space where fear dwells, anxiety is near. Choose to eliminate fear and let faith speak louder than the waves and winds of life. Before you start your day, choose to be fearless. Choose to be bold. Choose to crush timidity and stir up the gifts, talents, and abilities that are within you. Choose to go back to school. Choose to conquer that dream. Choose to launch that business. Choose to do what God has called you to do.

PRAYER

Father God, in the Name of Jesus, I surrender to You. Lord, remove any chains of fear that entangle my heart. Father, I choose to crush timidity and anything that's not like You. Father, I choose to submit to You.

Fear shall not dwell here. In the Name of Jesus, I rebuke the spirit of fear. Father, I choose to divorce myself from fear. Lord, lead my day.

In Jesus' Name. Amen.

Day 9

LAUNCH OUT INTO THE DEEP

Now when he had left speaking, he said unto Simon, Launch out into the deep, and let down your nets for a draught.

LUKE 5:4 KJV

Launch out into the deep and try again. Launch again and try something new. Stretch beyond the norm. Stretch beyond what's expected. Launch beyond the expectation and experience of others. Launch out and innovate. It's time to launch.

Luke 5:4 NLT declares, "When he had finished speaking, he said to Simon, Now go out where it is deeper, and let down your nets to catch some fish." Go out where it is deeper. It's time to go deeper spiritually. It's time to deepen your capacity to handle more. It's time to increase your ability to do more. It's time to launch. Launch and go out into the deep. It's time to catch a harvest.

Sometimes, your "catch" is in deep waters. Sometimes, your harvest is waiting for you when you go deeper. Sometimes, success is waiting on you in deep waters. Luke 5:4 NLT puts it this way, "When he had finished speaking, he said to Simon, Now go out where it is deeper, and let down your nets to catch some fish." Notice that Luke 5:4 NLT declares that in order to catch various types of fish you have to go into the deep.

Maybe, you've been living life in "shallow water". Maybe, you've been playing it safe and you've been staying close to the shore where it's comfortable. Pray, and ask God to take you deeper in every area of your life.

Maybe, you've been trying to catch fish while you're close to the shore. Maybe, you've been trying to get different results while you're still close to the shore. Luke 5:5 NLT declares, "Master, Simon replied, we worked hard all last night and didn't catch a thing. But if you say so, I'll let the nets down again."

Maybe, you feel like Peter and you've been working all night. Maybe, you've been toiling for years. However, as soon as Jesus spoke to Peter and spoke the word, "Launch", Peter's season immediately shifted. Through Peter's obedience he went from a season of toiling to a season of flourishing.

Luke 5:5 NLT declares, "Master, Simon replied, we worked hard all last night and didn't catch a thing. But if you say so, I'll let the nets down again." The King James Version puts it this way—"And Simon answering said unto him, Master, we have toiled all the night, and have taken nothing: nevertheless at thy word I will let down the net." "...Nevertheless at Your Word." "...But if You say so." Peter obeyed God. Peter obeyed Christ's instruction.

In order to shift from a season of mediocrity, failure, and defeat to a season of overflow and success, you have to submit to Christ. In order to shift from a season of toiling and lack to a season of prosperity and overflow, you have to kill pride and submit to Christ.

When Peter said, "Nevertheless at Your Word..." Peter killed pride. Peter killed his way and surrendered to Christ's Way. Peter admitted that his way was not working. Peter had been toiling all night. As soon as Peter surrendered to Christ his toiling season had ended.

Maybe you're skilled, maybe you're talented, maybe you're gifted, maybe you're experienced, maybe you're educated, maybe you're wealthy, and your way is still not working. Surrender your heart to Christ. Submit your hands to His timing. Surrender your heart to His "Launch". Surrender to God. His Way and His timing are perfect.

Peter was not only a skilled and experienced fisherman, he knew the appropriate time and the proper place to catch fish. But his way was not working. Maybe, you're an expert and you've been toiling all night. Maybe, you've been toiling for years. Choose to conquer your day by waiting for God's "Yes". Start your day by listening to the "Launch" of Christ. It's time to launch. Launch when Christ speaks. Launch on His "Yes".

What's stopping you from launching out into the deep? What are you afraid of? Is fear paralyzing you? Is fear choking your destiny? Is fear stunting your acts of faith? It takes faith to launch out into the deep. It takes wisdom to launch out where it's deeper. Choose to obey Christ and launch when He commands you to launch.

Launch out into the deep and execute mighty exploits for Christ. Launch that God-given dream. Launch that God-given vision. Launch that God-given business. Launch that God-given initiative. Launch in His season. Launch in His timing.

Notice what Peter declared in Luke 5:5 NLT, "Master, Simon replied, we worked hard all last night and didn't catch a thing. But if you say so, I'll let the nets down again." In other words Peter said, "Master, without You, we toiled and worked hard all night…"

Peter had gone fishing without Christ. He had toiled all night without Christ. Peter was skilled, Peter was experienced but yet Peter toiled. If Peter had taken Christ he would have saved time, energy, and effort. Don't launch without Christ. You may be skilled, you may be experienced, you may be talented but choose not to launch without Christ. Choose not to start your day without Christ. Conquer with Christ.

PRAYER

Father God, in the Name of Jesus, grant me the faith to launch into the deep. Father, lead me into deep waters.

Father, I choose to surrender to Your Word. Father, I choose to surrender to Your timing. Father, I choose to move forward upon Your Command.

Lord, I choose to follow Your Voice. Lead me upon the waters. Lead me to new territory. Father, order my steps.

Father, give me the courage to blaze new paths and walk into uncharted territories. Father, I am Yours forever.

In Jesus' Name. Amen.

Day 10

GO TO THE ANT

Go to the ant, thou sluggard; consider her ways, and be wise: Which having no guide, overseer, or ruler, Provideth her meat in the summer, and gathereth her food in the harvest.

PROVERBS 6:6-8 KJV

Diligence is required in this season. Choose to deploy diligence in every season of your life. Proverbs 6:6 KJV declares, "Go to the ant, thou sluggard; consider her ways, and be wise." Go to the ant and study its ways. Start your day by choosing to deploy diligence in every area of your life.

Notice the diligence principles outlined in Proverbs 6:6 KJV regarding the ant. The ant has no guide, no overseer, or ruler. Diligence matters. Self-governance matters. Steward your time well. Choose to diligently steward your job. Choose to steward the resources under your authority well.

The ant has no guide, meaning the ant does not need to be "micromanaged". The ant does not need a manager or an overseer. The ant's work ethic is impeccable. The ant is a self-starter. The ant initiates and stores food for the winter. In other words, the ant executes in the summer during "optimal time" and stores its food during harvest. Choose to execute in "Prime Time". Execute when God commands you to do so.

Take ownership of the opportunity. Steward the opportunity that God has given you. Steward the resources that God has given you. The ant gathers in harvest and executes in summer without having an overseer or ruler. Today, choose to execute consistently and diligently. Diligence is critical for your success.

Start your day with a mindset of diligence. Start your day by choosing to get things done. The ant has no overseer. The ant has no ruler. The ant has no manager. The ant is self-sufficient. The ant gathers and stores in seasons of plenty and has plenty to live on in winter. The ant gathers and has plenty to live on in times of scarcity. Now is the time to execute. Now is the time to gather. Now is the time to store.

Execute upon that God-given idea. Execute upon and launch that business. Take the next step. Execute and complete the tasks that are under your control. Today's execution positions future generations for success.

Your diligence, obedience, and execution today positions your house for future success. When you execute today and gather during harvest, seasons of scarcity will not take you off guard. Choose to execute today. Gather in harvest and enjoy the fruit of your diligence.

PRAYER

Father God, in the Name of Jesus, I thank You for this day. Lord, I will not mismanage this moment. Father, I ask You for the wisdom to steward the time that You have given me well.

Father, lead my steps. Lord, grant me the grace to execute diligently. Father, I ask that You grant me the wisdom to do what You've called me to do.

Lord, I ask that You grant me the grace to gather. Father, I ask that You grant me the grace to go above and beyond what is expected.

Lord, lead my path and guide my footsteps. Teach my hands to be diligent. Teach my heart to obey Your Voice. Father, Your Word is my shelter and I will forever surrender to You.

In Jesus' Name. Amen.

Day 11

ARISE OUT OF YOUR SLEEP

How long wilt thou sleep, O sluggard?
when wilt thou arise out of thy sleep?

PROVERBS 6:9 KJV

Don't waste the moment. Now is the time. When will you arise out of your sleep? When will you arise out of your slumber? There is never a perfect time to launch. Now is not the time to sleep. Now is not the time to slumber. Now is not the time to slack.

Your destiny is attached to your obedience. Your legacy is attached to your execution. Choose to execute upon that idea. Choose to execute upon that business. Choose to execute upon that God-given idea. Choose to move forward.

James 2:26 KJV declares, "For as the body without the spirit is dead, so faith without works is dead also." The Amplified Version expands upon James 2:26 AMPC in the following manner, "For as the human body apart from the spirit is lifeless, so faith apart from [its] works of obedience is also dead." Faith apart from obedience is dead.

In fact, James 2:20 KJV, puts it this way, "But wilt thou know, O vain man, that faith without works is dead?" Faith without works is dead. The Amplified Version expands upon James 2:20 in the following manner, "Are you willing to be shown [proof], you foolish (unproductive, spiritually deficient) fellow, that faith apart from [good] works is inactive and ineffective and worthless?"

The Bible declares that the foolish and vain are unproductive and spiritually deficient. Faith without works is inactive, ineffective, and worthless. Faith without progress towards the vision paralyzes your purpose. Work towards the vision. Work towards the goal. Philippians 3:14 KJV puts it this way, "I press toward the mark for the prize of the high calling of God in Christ Jesus." Choose to press towards the mark.

The Amplified Version expounds on Philippians 3:14 AMPC this way, "I press on toward the goal to win the [supreme and heavenly] prize to which God in Christ Jesus is calling us upward." Press towards the goal and despise not small beginnings.

Choose to start somewhere. Start with a benchmark. Establish a goal and press toward the mark. Choose to press and push daily. Don't waste the moment. Don't let the headwinds of life stop you from moving forward. Keep moving forward. Don't let the headwinds of life stop your momentum. Arise out of your sleep and move forward. Arise out of your slumber and execute.

Ask God for witty ideas and innovative strategies to push past obstacles. Arise out of making excuses. Choose to execute. Choose to do what God has told you to do. If you don't know where to start, choose to execute by seeking God, pray, and take the first step. Every marathon begins with the "first step". Take the first step. Despise not your small steps. Despise not your small beginnings. Choose to take that first step in faith. Every first step requires faith.

In fact, every step you take requires faith. 2 Corinthians 5:7 KJV declares, "For we walk by faith, not by sight." Choose to walk by faith and not by what you see. For every small step you take today paves the way for future generations. Before you start your day, choose to make the decision to walk and diligently execute by faith. Let nothing stand in your way and walk by faith.

PRAYER

Father God, in the Name of Jesus, I thank You for the opportunity to serve and honor You. Father, I will not waste this moment. Father, I will steward the opportunity that You have given me.

Father, I will not sleep and procrastinate during my season of execution. Father, lead my path. Father, I will choose to execute. Father, I will not slack. Father, I will not slumber. Father, I will not delay. Father, I choose to course correct and I will execute upon the God-given idea that You've given me.

Father, I will execute upon Your Command. Lord, I will obey Your Voice. Father, I choose to follow You. Lord, I surrender my heart to You.

In Jesus' Name. Amen.

Day 12

THE THOUGHTS OF THE DILIGENT

The thoughts of the diligent tend only to plenteousness; but of every one that is hasty only to want.

PROVERBS 21:5 KJV

The thoughts of the diligent tend only to plenty. Even the "way" you think has an impact on how you start your day. Proverbs 21:5 AMPC declares, "The thoughts of the [steadily] diligent tend only to plenteousness, but everyone who is impatient and hasty hastens only to want."

The thoughts of the steadily diligent leads to success. Your "Thought Life" has purpose. The thoughts of the steadily diligent leads to plenty. But those who are impatient and hasty leads to lack. Let God lead your thoughts. Let His Word shape and develop the framework and details of your day. Let God lead the framework of your life.

Proverbs 21:5 NLT puts it this way, "Good planning and hard work lead to prosperity, but hasty shortcuts lead to poverty." Choose to plan. Plan out your day. Diligently plan out your daily execution. Diligently plan out what success looks like. Plan to succeed. Plan to exceed your goals. Set a benchmark and press toward the goal. Then surpass it.

Proverbs 18:20 KJV declares, "A man's belly shall be satisfied with the fruit of his mouth; and with the increase of his lips shall he be filled." Choose to set your mouth on success. Choose to fill your mouth with His Word. The Amplified Version puts Proverbs 18:20 AMPC in the following manner, "A man's [moral] self shall be filled with the fruit of his mouth; and with the consequence of his words he must be satisfied [whether good or evil]." Choose to set your heart and your mouth on success. Choose to speak life. Choose to set your heart and your mind on His Word.

Surround yourself with those who are speaking life. Surround yourself with those who are concerned about executing upon their God-given purpose. Surround yourself with those who choose to do things God's Way.

Psalm 1:1 AMPC declares, "BLESSED (HAPPY, fortunate, prosperous, and enviable) is the man who walks and lives not in the counsel of the ungodly [following their advice, their plans and purposes], nor stands [submissive and inactive] in the path where sinners walk, nor sits down [to relax and rest] where the scornful [and the mockers] gather."

Choose not to follow after the counsel of the ungodly. Choose not to follow after the advice, plans, and purposes of the ungodly. Choose not to follow after the path of the inactive. Choose not to be submissive and inactive in the path where sinners walk. Choose to walk by faith and surround yourself with Godly counselors.

Choose to surround yourself with those who pattern themselves after a lifestyle of diligence. Surround yourself with mature counselors who are wise, seasoned, conditioned, and consistent.

Before you start your day, ask God to surround you with mature mentors who can help lead and guide the steps of your destiny. Ask God to lead you to the right counselors. Ask God to lead you to the right mentors.

The diligent are focused. The diligent are intentional. The diligent are disciplined. The diligent are determined. Don't let the weight of the world distract you from fulfilling your purpose. Choose to conquer the winds and waves of life by trusting in God. Choose to navigate and conquer the storm by relying on His Word.

Joshua 1:7-9 AMPC declares, "Only you be strong and very courageous, that you may do according to all the law which Moses My servant commanded you. Turn not from it to the right hand or to the left, that you may prosper wherever you go. This Book of the Law shall not depart out of your mouth, but you shall meditate on it day and night, that you may observe and do according to all that is written in it. For then you shall make your way prosperous, and then you shall deal wisely and have good success. Have not I commanded you? Be strong, vigorous, and very courageous. Be not afraid, neither be dismayed, for the Lord your God is with you wherever you go."

Don't look to your left or to your right, focus on Christ. Be strong, vigorous, and very courageous. Be not afraid, neither be dismayed, for the Lord your God is with you wherever you go. Focus on Christ. Diligently focus on the goal at hand and let Christ lead your course.

PRAYER

Father God, in the Name of Jesus, I thank You for the courage to diligently pursue everything that You've called me to do. Father,

I will steward today well. Father, I will diligently focus on my assignment and steward the opportunity that You have given me.

Father, I will not waste this moment. Father, I will not waste the time that you have given me. Father I will steward my "Thought Life" and focus on You. Lord, I will not look to the left or to the right—I will not be distracted by the waves and winds.

Father, I choose to trust You. I choose to surrender my heart to You. Father, I choose to surrender my day to You. Father, I choose to surrender my ways to You. My eyes are fixed on You. My eyes are fixed on the goal. My eyes are fixed on my purpose.

In Jesus' Name. Amen.

Day 13

THE HAND OF THE DILIGENT

"The hand of the diligent shall bear rule."
but the slothful shall be under tribute.

PROVERBS 12:24 KJV

Diligence is critical for the next level. In order to move to the next level, deploy diligence. In order to move to the next season, deploy diligence. Before you start your day, let diligence surround every aspect of your life.

The New International Version (NIV), puts Proverbs 12:24 in the following manner, "Diligent hands will rule, but laziness ends in forced labor." Diligent and consistent hands will lead and rule but laziness will end in forced labor. Diligent and consistent processes will lead and rule but the slothful will end in forced labor.

Choose to be diligent. Choose to start. Start small if you have to. Eliminate slack and deploy consistent diligence in every area of your life. Deploy diligence in business. Deploy diligence and strengthen your spiritual life. Deploy diligence and strengthen your family. Deploy diligence and execute in excellence on your job. Whether it's diligently exercising, consistently praying, or diligently writing that book, choose to deploy diligence in every area of your life. Choose to integrate diligence in every aspect of your day.

Proverbs 24:30-34 KJV declares, "I went by the field of the slothful, and by the vineyard of the man void of understanding; And, lo, it was all grown over with thorns, and nettles had covered the face thereof, and the stone wall thereof was broken down. Then I saw, and considered it well: I looked upon it, and received instruction. Yet a little sleep, a little slumber, a little folding of the hands to sleep: So shall thy poverty come as one that travelleth; and thy want as an armed man."

The field of the slothful is covered by thorns and weeds. In other words, the slothful do not steward their resources well. In fact, the slothful mishandles the opportunities afforded to them. The slothful mishandles the financial resources under their care. The thorns and weeds described in Proverbs 24:31 represent the neglected areas of the lazy person's life.

When an area of one's life is neglected for so long, it soon corrodes and crumbles. If you neglect the responsibilities on your job for so long, it will soon corrode and crumble. If you're financially slothful and neglect your fiscal responsibilities, the thorns and weeds represent past due bills, and consistently having past-due bills will soon corrode your financial health.

Choose not to be lazy in any area of your life. Choose not to be fiscally lazy. Choose not to be emotionally slothful. Choose to diligently handle the heart of your family. Don't let the thorns and weeds of unresolved issues corrode the emotional integrity of your family. Don't let thorns and weeds of unresolved bills corrode the financial integrity of your house.

Proverbs 24:30-34 NIV declares, "I went past the field of a sluggard, past the vineyard of someone who has no sense; thorns had come up everywhere, the ground was covered with weeds, and the stone wall was in ruins. I applied my heart to what I observed and learned a lesson from what I saw: A little sleep, a little slumber, a little folding of the hands to rest — and poverty will come on you like a thief and scarcity like an armed man."

Don't "sleep on" or ignore emotional matters that require your attention or they will cause your stone wall, the emotional infrastructure of your home, to crumble. The slothful or the sluggard will choose to ignore problems that need to be addressed. Choose to be diligent and execute. Choose to address problems and issues that require your attention.

Whether financially, spiritually, emotionally, physically, or mentally—choose to diligently address issues before they fester and grow into larger problems. Develop a plan and execute upon it. Proverbs 21:5 NLT declares, "Good planning and hard work lead to prosperity, but hasty shortcuts lead to poverty." Diligently cultivate your field. Execute upon your assignments. Eliminate all excuses. Take no shortcuts in this season.

TODAY'S ACTION

- Decide to eliminate all excuses.
- No shortcuts. Eliminate every slothful shortcut in your life.
- Be intentional. Set a goal for today and decide to accomplish it. In fact, exceed the goal that you've set.

Day 14

THE SLOTHFUL DOES NOT ROAST

The slothful man roasteth not that which he took in hunting: but the substance of a diligent man is precious.

PROVERBS 12:27 KJV

The slothful do not complete assignments. The slothful wastes the opportunity presented to them. The slothful does not take full advantage of every opportunity afforded to them. Proverbs 12:27 NLT puts it this way, "Lazy people don't even cook the game they catch, but the diligent make use of everything they find."

The lazy do not roast the opportunity presented to them, but the diligent make use of each and every opportunity and every season. God has given you the gift of "today". Choose to steward today well.

The diligent choose to steward the resources presented to them well. The diligent makes use of every opportunity. Steward your moment well. Steward your opportunity well. Steward your platform well. Steward the resources under your care well.

God has given you gifts, talents, opportunities, and platforms to steward and oversee. The slothful choose not to fully pursue the opportunities presented to them. The diligent make use of everything under their authority. Steward your moment. Diligently steward your time. Steward your resources well.

The slothful do not fully value the opportunities presented to them. In fact, the slothful makes excuses. Choose not to make excuses. There are many who are able to "win" with the "hand" that you've been "dealt". There are many who will win with what's in your hand. What's holding you back from pursuing everything that God has for you?

Diligence is required for your next level. Diligence is required for growth. Diligence is required for personal development. Diligence is required for success. Don't leave projects halfway completed. Choose to set your goal and complete the assignment.

Psalm 1:1-3 KJV declares, "Blessed is the man that walketh not in the counsel of the ungodly, nor standeth in the way of sinners, nor sitteth in the seat of the scornful. But his delight is in the law of the Lord; and in his law doth he meditate day and night. And he shall be like a tree planted by the rivers of water, that bringeth forth his fruit in his season; his leaf also shall not wither; and whatsoever he doeth shall prosper."

Those who stay diligent will produce fruit in his season. Those who choose to diligently treasure and apply God's Word in every area of their life will not wither. The leaf of the diligent will not wither. No matter what season comes their way, the diligent will not wither because they are nourished and sustained by their deep roots.

The slothful take the "training" seasons of the past for granted. When it's time to be taught, the slothful do not digest and apply the principles and lessons that need to be learned. The slothful sporadically executes and does not get consistent results.

The diligent draws from past lessons. The diligent draws from past teachings. The diligent draws from past testimonies. Choose to roast every lesson. Choose to diligently meditate on His Word and learn from your past mistakes. Choose to diligently meditate on His Word and learn from the past mistakes of others.

Surround yourself with wise, mature, and seasoned counselors. Surround yourself with those who are not spiritually lazy. Surround yourself with those who are not emotional sluggards. Surround yourself with those who want to grow and develop. Surround yourself with those who are not financially lazy.

Decide to surround yourself with those who choose to roast the resources and opportunities presented to them. Today, choose to intentionally decide to surround yourself with those who "roast". Like the ant, decide to gather in the summer. Be diligent and roast what you've gathered. It's time to gather. It's time to roast. It's time to execute.

TODAY'S ACTION

- Reflect on the lessons of the past. Choose to reflect on past wins. Choose to learn from past losses.
- Pray and ask God to surround yourself with wise Godly counselors.
- Surround yourself with those mature mentors who have sat in the seat that you're looking to occupy.

Day 15

THE SOUL OF THE SLUGGARD

The soul of the sluggard desireth, and hath nothing: but the soul of the diligent shall be made fat.

PROVERBS 13:4 KJV

The soul of the sluggard desires and have nothing. The soul of the sluggard have dreams and accomplishes nothing. Proverbs 13:4 AMPC declares, "The appetite of the sluggard craves and gets nothing, but the appetite of the diligent is abundantly supplied."

The soul of the diligent shall be made fat. The diligent are abundantly supplied. The diligent are surrounded by those who are diligent. Proverbs 11:14 KJV declares, "Where no counsel is, the people fall: but in the multitude of counsellors there is safety." There's safety when you surround yourself with a multitude of wise and seasoned counselors.

Who are your counselors? Surround yourself with those who have a mindset of diligence. Proverbs 13:4 NLT puts it this way, "Lazy people want much but get little, but those who work hard will prosper." Surround yourself with those who are diligent. Surround yourself with those who will work hard.

Surround yourself with those who are not afraid to put their hands to the plow. Luke 9:62 KJV declares, "And Jesus said unto him, No man, having put his hand to the plough, and looking back, is fit for the kingdom of God." Keep your hands on the plow. Don't become slothful. Keep plowing. Keep going. Don't stop. Don't look back. Don't make excuses. Keep executing.

Proverbs 13:4 NLT declares, "Lazy people want much but get little, but those who work hard will prosper." Lazy people will not plow. They desire harvest but they refuse to plow. The lazy desire harvest but refuse to cultivate their garden. The lazy desire but have nothing. The slothful have grandiose dreams but refuse to plow. You choose.

Plow your land. Plow the opportunity that God has given you. Plow your heart with the Word of God and remove anything that's not like Him. Jeremiah 4:3 KJV declares, "For thus saith the Lord to the men of Judah and Jerusalem, Break up your fallow ground, and sow not among thorns."

Sow not among thorns. Sow not your valuable information, revelation, insight, wisdom, and time amongst those who do not value what you're pouring out. Jeremiah 4:3 NLT puts it this way, "This is what the Lord says to the people of Judah and Jerusalem: "Plow up the hard ground of your hearts! Do not waste your good seed among thorns." Don't waste your seed among thorns. Thorny hearts choke your time, resources, and energy.

2 Corinthians 9:10 AMPC declares, "And [God] Who provides seed for the sower and bread for eating will also provide and multiply your [resources for] sowing and increase the fruits of your righteousness [which manifests itself in active goodness, kindness, and charity]." God gives seed to the sower. God gives seed to the one who selflessly sows.

He gives spiritual seed (wisdom, insight, and revelation) to the sower. He gives you more revelation (seed) to those who sow revelation into others. God increases your capability and capacity to those who sow into others. Don't hoard the gifts that God has given you. Choose to start your day by becoming a sower. Sow into others.

Choose to invest in others. Choose to build up others. Use the gifts, talents, resources, wisdom, insight, and abilities that God has given you to strengthen others. Diligently sow into others. Diligently pour into others. Sluggards choose to withhold their "pour". The lazy choose to withhold sowing into others. Don't procrastinate.

Don't selfishly withhold your gifts, time, and talent—pour into others. God gives seed to the diligent. Don't waste the seed. Don't waste the moment. Don't waste the opportunity. The ways of the diligent shall prosper. It's time to pour. It's time to selflessly pour into others.

TODAY'S ACTION

- Do you have a mindset of diligence? Cultivate a work ethic and pattern of diligence in every area of your life.

- Put your hands to the plow. Surround yourself with those who will work hard. Decide to execute and move forward. Don't look back.

- Don't withhold your talent. Don't withhold your gifts. Intentionally pour into others. Mentor someone. Sharpen someone. Sow into others. Who are you sharpening?

Day 16

SEEST THOU A MAN DILIGENT IN HIS BUSINESS?

Seest thou a man diligent in his business? he shall stand before kings; he shall not stand before mean men.

PROVERBS 22:29 KJV

Remove slack and become diligent. The diligent shall bear rule. The diligent shall lead others. The diligent shall prosper. The diligent shall stand before kings. Are you diligent?

Are you diligent in business? Are you diligent in your business affairs? Are you diligent on your job? Are you diligent in ministry? Do you diligently steward the gifts, talents, resources, platforms, and opportunities that God has given you?

Proverbs 22:29 KJV declares that those who are diligent, shall stand before kings. Those who are diligent shall stand before people of influence. Those who are diligent shall stand before those who are in authority. Are you diligent?

If you want to measure your level of diligence in an area, check to see who you are serving. Who are you standing before? Are you standing before kings? Are you presenting before kings? If you want to check to see if you're diligent in an area, check your "Diligence Barometer". A barometer, is defined as, "An instrument measuring atmospheric pressure, used especially in forecasting the weather and determining altitude."

Let's examine the first part of the definition—"a barometer is an instrument measuring atmospheric pressure". One way to check your level of diligence is to check your atmospheric pressure. How high are you in your organization? How high are you going within an organization? How influential are you within your organization?

Please note, and be mindful, that your title or position alone does not determine your level of diligence. There are some mid-level managers who outperform some executives. Your position alone is not a permanent determinant of your level of diligence—it's simply an indicator.

In fact, according to the latter portion of the definition, a barometer is used especially in "forecasting the weather and determining altitude". Diligence is a forecasting element of success. In fact, the second definition of a barometer is, "Something which reflects changes in circumstances or opinions." Diligence will change your circumstance.

Apply diligence to any area of slack. Apply diligence to any area of lack. Apply diligence to any underperforming area. Apply diligence to any area that needs attention. Proverbs 22:29 NLT declares, "Do you see any truly competent workers? They will serve kings rather than working for ordinary people." Apply diligence and you will not serve ordinary people; you will serve kings. Apply diligence and you will not be ordinary.

Proverbs 22:29 AMPC declares, "Do you see a man diligent and skillful in his business? He will stand before kings; he will not stand before obscure men." Apply diligence and you will not serve obscure men; you will serve those of authority.

Notice what Proverbs 22:29 AMPC declares, "Do you see a man diligent and skillful in business." The Amplified Version adds the word "skillful" in addition to diligence. What's your expertise? Are you skilled in an area? If you find yourself slacking in an area or underperforming in an area, choose to diligently develop that skill and sharpen your skill set.

Before you start your day, choose to focus on a weak area of your life. Select an area of "opportunity" and find ways to improve that weak or target area. Choose to set small incremental goals, set markers, and celebrate milestones. Make progress. Put a process in place to press toward the mark until you have reached your goal.

Diligently focus on a weak area and progress towards fulfilling the goal. Progress is not perfection. Progress towards your goal. Diligently press towards the mark. Diligence will strengthen your weak areas and will transform your weaknesses into strengths.

Choose to build your skill set. Choose to sharpen your skills and you will always be in demand. Proverbs 22:29 MSG declares, "Observe people who are good at their work— skilled workers are always in demand and admired; they don't take a backseat to anyone."

TODAY'S ACTION

- Before you start your day, choose to focus on a weak area of your life.
- Select an area of "opportunity" and find ways to improve upon that target area.

- Proverbs 27:17 KJV declares, "Iron sharpeneth iron; so a man sharpeneth the countenance of his friend." Surround yourself with "Iron-Sharpening" Counsel. Surround yourself with those who are willing to "sharpen" and strengthen you.

Day 17

KNOW THE STATE OF THY FLOCKS

Be thou diligent to know the state of thy flocks, and look well to thy herds.

PROVERBS 27:23 KJV

Before you start your day, know the state of thy flocks. Proverbs 27:23 KJV is a scripture that refers to the diligent stewardship of resources. Back in Biblical days, "flocks and herds" were considered as the main source of income and revenue streams to many farming families. In fact, "flocks" were a valuable "asset class" and used as a point of exchange for many.

In today's capitalistic society, "flocks and herds" are a reference to "real assets". Before you start your day, be diligent and know the state of thy assets. Proverbs 27:23 AMPC puts it this way, "Be diligent to know the state of your flocks, and look well to your herds." Look well to your herds. Look well to your entire portfolio.

Diligently look over the resources under your care. Whether it's real estate, stocks, bonds, mutual funds, bank accounts, investment accounts, retirement accounts etc., know the state of thy flocks and thy herds.

If diligently taking care of your finances is a daunting task, choose to engage experts. Surround yourself with financial advisors and/or financial mentors who have financial expertise in various areas. Proverbs 27:23 NLT declares, "Know the state of your flocks, and put your heart into caring for your herds," Put your heart into caring for the assets under your care.

Proverbs 27:23 NIV puts it this way, "Be sure you know the condition of your flocks, give careful attention to your herds." Give careful attention to your accounts. In order to advance to your next level, pay careful attention to what's in your hand today.

Can God trust you with more resources? Can God trust you with more capital? Can God trust you with more responsibility? Can God give you more seed? If God enlarged the resources under your care, would you lose more or will you multiply the resources under your stewardship?

Remember, God gives seed to the sower. He gives resources to those whom He trusts. He gives more seed to those who properly steward the resources under their care. God gives more seed to those who carefully tend to their flock.

Proverbs 27:23-27 MSG expounds on this stewardship principle in the following manner, "Know your sheep by name; carefully attend to your flocks; (Don't take them for granted; possessions don't last forever, you know.) And then, when the crops are in and the harvest is stored in the barns, You can knit sweaters from lambs' wool, and sell your goats for a profit; There will be plenty of milk and meat to last your family through the winter."

Carefully tend to the resources that are under your care today so that there will be plenty of milk and meat (resources) to last your family through the winter. God wants you to steward the resources under your care. Diligently steward the resources and the opportunities that are under your care today, so that when "winter" comes you'll have plenty of resources to survive the season of famine.

Know the state of thy flocks and don't take them for granted. Don't take your income and revenue streams for granted. Study, protect, steward, and multiply the various streams of income, resources, revenue, and assets under your care. "Be thou diligent to know the state of thy flocks, and look well to thy herds." Proverbs 27:23 KJV. Study your flocks and know thy herds.

TODAY'S ACTION

- Before you start your day, know the state of thy flocks. Study your income and revenue streams. Monitor your investments.
- Create a budget. Make a financial plan.
- If financial affairs intimidate you, find, interview, and consult a financial advisor and surround yourself with those who are fiscally responsible.
- Start reading financial books and resources that can increase your financial exposure and awareness.

Day 18

BEFORE YOU BUILD

For which of you, intending to build a tower, sitteth not down first, and counteth the cost, whether he have sufficient to finish it?

LUKE 14:28 KJV

Before you start a major project, sit down, and count the cost. Before you leap into a major project, sit down, with wise counsel, and plan. Consider the cost. Before you start a new career, sit down, surround yourself with wise counselors, and mature mentors and plan your career path. Before you start a new business, sit down, surround yourself with wise counselors and mature business mentors and weigh the cost.

Before you build, engage God. Before you build, engage wise counsel. Before you start anything, engage God and consult with wise counselors who are skilled and have the Heart of God. Pattern yourself after Christ's Way of doing things. Choose to follow His Word, pattern your execution after His Command, and get His results.

Proverbs 16:3 KJV declares, "Commit thy works unto the Lord, and thy thoughts shall be established." Proverbs 16:3 AMPC expounds on it this way, "Roll your works upon the

Lord [commit and trust them wholly to Him; He will cause your thoughts to become agreeable to His will, and] so shall your plans be established and succeed." Roll your works upon the Lord. Let His Word lead your heart.

Surrender your heart to Christ and He will guide your footsteps. Psalm 37:23 KJV declares, "The steps of a good man are ordered by the Lord: and he delighteth in his way." The New Living Translation expounds on Psalm 37:23 NLT in the following manner, "The Lord directs the steps of the godly. He delights in every detail of their lives."

God delights in every detail of your life. Before you start your day, know that He cares about every detail of your life. Before you start your day, know that God cares about the financial details of your life. Before you start your day, know that God cares about the success of your career. Before you start your day, know that God cares about the success of your business.

Before you start your day, know that God cares about the health and condition of your heart and soul. 3 John 1:2 KJV declares, "Beloved, I wish above all things that thou mayest prosper and be in health, even as thy soul prospereth." 3 John 1:2 AMPC expounds on it this way, "Beloved, I pray that you may prosper in every way and [that your body] may keep well, even as [I know] your soul keeps well and prospers."

John 10:10 AMPC declares, "The thief comes only in order to steal and kill and destroy. I came that they may have and enjoy life, and have it in abundance (to the full, till it overflows)." Christ cares about your spiritual and natural needs. Christ came so that you might have and enjoy life, and have it in abundance, to the full, till it overflows.

Christ wants you to succeed in every area of your life. God does not want you to fail. So before you start your day, before you build, engage with the Builder of Heaven and Earth. Engage with the One who created time itself. Before you build, consult with God, the Author of your purpose and destiny.

Jeremiah 1:5 KJV declares, "Before I formed thee in the belly I knew thee; and before thou camest forth out of the womb I sanctified thee, and I ordained thee a prophet unto the nations." Before you were formed God knew you. Before you were crafted and created, God had an intimate relationship with you.

God strategically planted you in the Earth. God intentionally created you. God placed you in this moment in time for a reason. So each day has purpose. Each day has significance. Each moment has purpose. God does not make mistakes and He wants to lead and guide your day. Surrender your day to God. Surrender your moment to Him. Before you start your day, surrender your day over to Him.

Understand and know that God created time itself and He occupies every aspect of time—He is Omnipresent. So before you start "your" day, the day that He's given to you, know that He's already there. Jeremiah 23:24 KJV declares, "Can any hide himself in secret places that I shall not see him? saith the Lord. Do not I fill heaven and earth? saith the Lord."

God fills all of Heaven and Earth. He fills every void, gap, and deficit. He occupies all space and all of time—for all of eternity. So don't worry about today, know that God is already there. He already occupies every moment. Surrender your moment to God.

TODAY'S ACTION

- Before you build anything, pray and ask God for wisdom and direction. Count the cost, examine the risk, and make a plan to achieve success.

- Before you make any life-altering decisions, surround yourself with and consult wise counsel.

Day 19

DON'T LOOK BACK

And he overthrew those cities, and all the plain, and all the inhabitants of the cities, and that which grew upon the ground. But his wife looked back from behind him, and she became a pillar of salt.

GENESIS 19:25-26 KJV

In Genesis Chapter 19, God overthrew the cities of Sodom and Gomorrah. When God overthrows something, it's for a purpose. Before you start your day, don't pick back up what God has overthrown. Don't pick back up the things of yesterday. Don't pick up the old things.

Don't pick back up the old man. Let the old man go. Let the old processes go. Let stagnation go. Let the pain of the past go. Let the chains of the past go. Let heartache go. Let old habits go. Let the shame and condemnation of the past go. Let guilt go. Let disobedience go. Let slothful behaviors go. Let laziness go. Let every ungodly "soul tie" go. Divorce yourself from the things of the past. Let God clean your heart and give you a fresh start.

In fact, today, at this very moment, when you surrender to Christ, you have a fresh start in Him. Choose to surrender your day to Christ. When God overthrows a thing, don't turn back.

Don't look back. When God does a brand new thing in your life, don't turn back to the things of old.

Proverbs 26:11 KJV puts it this way, "As a dog returneth to his vomit, so a fool returneth to his folly." Fools return to their folly. Don't return to the old man. Returning back to the old man is like returning to vomit. Don't consume things that God has rejected. Don't return to your old habits. Don't return to the old cravings of the past. Don't return to the appetite of the past.

Genesis 19:26 KJV declares, "But his wife looked back from behind him, and she became a pillar of salt." Genesis 19:26 KJV shows us what happens when you look back at the things that God has overthrown. When you look back and desire to cling to the perversion of the past your heart becomes stagnant. In fact, focusing on the old things, the old ways, and old habits of the past will paralyze your destiny.

Notice, when Lot's wife turned back, she became a pillar of salt. Notice, her entire body remained stuck in the place of her disobedience. She turned back to the past. She desired the things that God had overthrown. Her heart longed for the things that God abhorred. When you desire to follow after idols and the things of this world your heart becomes stagnant and stuck to the things of the past.

Psalm 115:3-9 KJV puts it this way, "But our God is in the heavens: he hath done whatsoever he hath pleased. Their idols are silver and gold, the work of men's hands. They have mouths, but they speak not: eyes have they, but they see not: They have ears, but they hear not: noses have they, but they smell not: They have hands, but they handle not: feet have they, but they walk not: neither speak they through their throat. They that make them are like unto them; so is every that trusteth in them. O Israel, trust thou in the Lord: he is their help and their shield."

But our God is in the Heavens, He is the True and Living God. The idols of the world are made of silver and gold; they are the manipulated work of men's hands. Lot's wife's heart longed for the idols of Sodom and Gomorrah. She wanted to serve the things that God had destroyed. Lot's wife was stuck on the things of yesterday, while Lot and the rest of the family were moving forward.

Lot and his family were being led out of bondage, but Lot's wife chose to stay stuck in the old framework of the past. Don't stay stuck in the old framework of the past. Move forward in freedom. Embrace the new things. Live in the present. Press forward towards the mark. Look towards God and trust Him. Don't look back. Don't cling on to the transgressions of the past. Psalm 103:12 KJV declares, "As far as the east is from the west, so far hath he removed our transgressions from us."

Romans 8:1 KJV declares, "There is therefore now no condemnation to them which are in Christ Jesus, who walk not after the flesh, but after the Spirit." There is no condemnation to those who follow Christ. Before you start your day, let the condemnation of the past go. Before you start your day, let the guilt of the past go. Before you start your day, let the shame of yesterday go.

"Therefore if any man be in Christ, he is a new creature: old things are passed away; behold, all things are become new." 2 Corinthians 5:17 KJV. In Christ you are a new creature. Surrender your heart to God. Submit to His Way of doing things and let the things of the past go. Look forward. Look to the future. Look to Christ.

PRAYER

Father God, in the Name of Jesus, I turn to You. Father, You are the True and Living God. Lord, I surrender every aspect of my life over to You. Father, I surrender every area of my heart to You.

Father, I choose to serve You alone. Father, there is no one like You. Father, guide my heart. Lord, lead my footsteps. Lord, I look to You. My heart will not look back to the idols of past generations.

Lord, I fully surrender to You. Father, I choose not to serve any false idols. My life will honor you. I will not look back and focus on the past.

In Jesus' Name. Amen.

Day 20

HARDEN NOT YOUR HEART

Harden not your heart, as in the provocation, and as in the day of temptation in the wilderness

PSALMS 95:8 KJV

Harden not your heart. Let God soften every area of your heart. Let God wash every part of your heart. Psalm 95:8 NLT declares, "The Lord says, "Don't harden your hearts as Israel did at Meribah, as they did at Massah in the wilderness." According to Strong's Concordance, the Hebrew word, "meribah" (H4809) means, "Strife or contention".

Before you start your day, let God heal every area of your heart. Don't stay stuck in the contention of the past. Don't stay stuck in the strife of yesterday. Don't stay stuck in the wilderness of yesterday. Don't stay stuck in the bondage of the past. Don't stay stuck in the prison of the past.

The children of Israel stayed stuck in the wilderness, for longer than they had to, because of the strife and contention held in their hearts. Strife will keep your heart bound to the offense of the past. Strife will harden your heart. Contention will harden your heart from the inside out. God wants you to have a soft, pliable, and submitted heart. Surrender your heart to Him.

Matthew 11:28 AMPC declares, "Come to Me, all you who labor and are heavy-laden and overburdened, and I will cause you to rest. [I will ease and relieve and refresh your souls.]" Let Christ give you rest. In fact, before you start your day, let God give you a new heart.

Ezekiel 36:26 KJV declares, "A new heart also will I give you, and a new spirit will I put within you: and I will take away the stony heart out of your flesh, and I will give you an heart of flesh." Let God give you a heart of flesh. Let God transplant that heart of stone for a pliable and submitted heart of flesh.

Psalm 95:8 NLT declares, "The Lord says, "Don't harden your hearts as Israel did at Meribah, as they did at Massah in the wilderness." According to Strong's Concordance, the Hebrew word, "massah" (H4532) means, "temptation". Don't let your heart be tempted to become hardened while you're going through the wilderness.

Psalm 23:4 KJV puts it this way, "Yea, though I walk through the valley of the shadow of death, I will fear no evil: for thou art with me; thy rod and thy staff they comfort me." The wilderness is not a permanent place of habitation. Go through the wilderness. Don't prolong your journey. The wilderness is only for a season.

The children of Israel were only supposed to go through the wilderness for a few days. They prolonged their journey due to their disobedience. They wandered in the wilderness for forty years because of the contention held in their hearts. Don't stay stuck in a place because of the condition of your heart. The wilderness was not meant to destroy you. The wilderness was not meant to harm you. The wilderness was meant to expose what's in your heart.

Jesus Christ went through the wilderness for forty days and He set the example on how to conquer the wilderness. Christ became "The Wilderness Blueprint". If you're ever faced with a wilderness season, look to Christ. Jesus set the example as to how to defeat the wilderness.

Christ is more powerful than the wilderness that you face. Your purpose is bigger than the wilderness. Your assignment is bigger than the wilderness that you face. When you're going through the wilderness, don't look to the left or to the right—look to Christ. Let His Light, light your path.

John 14:6 KJV declares, "Jesus saith unto him, I am the way, the truth, and the life: no man cometh unto the Father, but by me." He is the Way. If you're facing a wilderness—choose to rely on God. He is the Way out. He will make a way when there is no way. Let God carve out a new way. Let His Light shine brighter than the wilderness that you face.

Isaiah 43:19 KJV declares, "Behold, I will do a new thing; now it shall spring forth; shall ye not know it? I will even make a way in the wilderness, and rivers in the desert." Before you start your day, let God do a new thing. Let God do the miraculous. Let God do the impossible. Let God show Himself mighty in the middle of the dead and dry valley.

PRAYER

Father God, in the Name of Jesus, soften every area of my heart. Father, cultivate the ground of my heart. Lord, my heart will not wither in the wilderness.

Lord, wash every part of my heart. Lord, lead my heart. Father, I refuse to complain. Lord, I refuse to grow bitter. Lord,

I choose to trust You. Father, I will not magnify the wilderness above Your Authority.

Lord, You are more powerful than the wilderness that I face. Lord, You are more powerful than the famine. Lord, You are mightier than the desert. Father, I refuse to be distracted by the waves and storms of life. Father, I look to You to light my path.

In Jesus' Name. Amen.

Day 21

KEEP YOUR HEART WITH ALL DILIGENCE

*Keep thy heart with all diligence;
for out of it are the issues of life.*

PROVERBS 4:23 KJV

Proverbs 4:23 NLT declares, "Guard your heart above all else, for it determines the course of your life." Guard your heart with the Word of God. Guard, protect, and keep your heart above all else, for it determines the course of your life. The condition of your ground and the soil of your heart determines the course of your life. Before you start your day, remember to nourish the ground of your heart with His Word.

Galatians 5:1 AMPC declares, "IN [this] freedom Christ has made us free [and completely liberated us]; stand fast then, and do not be hampered and held ensnared and submit again to a yoke of slavery [which you have once put off]." Christ has made you free. Christ has completely liberated you from the bondage of the past. Don't be hampered and ensnared by the chains of the past. Don't be hampered and ensnared by the yokes of the past.

Before you start your day, guard your heart with the Word of God. Cultivate and groom the ground of your heart with His

Word. Let the issues and pressures of life be guarded by His Word. Proverbs 4:23 AMPC declares, "Keep and guard your heart with all vigilance and above all that you guard, for out of it flow the springs of life." Keep your heart with all vigilance. Don't let the cares, worries, and entanglements of life choke your harvest.

Don't let the cares of this world strangle your destiny. Stay focused on the assignment at hand. Stay diligent. Look forward. Look to Christ who is the Author and Finisher of your faith. He is the Author and Finisher of our day. He is the Author and Finisher of our destiny. He is the Potter and we are His clay. We are dust formed by His Hand.

He cares about every intricate detail of your life. He cares about your family affairs. He cares about your emotional and mental health. He cares about your financial health. He cares about your physical health. He cares about every part of your life. Before you start your day, know that He cares about every moment of your day. He is vehemently concerned about you.

Proverbs 4:23-27 NIV declares, "Above all else, guard your heart, for everything you do flows from it. Keep your mouth free of perversity; keep corrupt talk far from your lips. Let your eyes look straight ahead; fix your gaze directly before you. Give careful thought to the paths for your feet and be steadfast in all your ways. Do not turn to the right or the left; keep your foot from evil." Keep your heart with all diligence. Do not turn to the right or the left. Stay focused. Keep your heart free of perverse talk. Keep your mouth free of corrupt communication. Before you start your day, surrender every aspect of it over to Christ the Author and Ruler of every age.

PRAYER

Father God, in the Name of Jesus, I thank You for Your Word. Lord, Your Word guards my life. Father, Your Word guides my heart. Father, Your Word leads and guides my footsteps. Father, Your Word orders my day. Father, I thank You that Your Word leads and guides every aspect of my life. Lord, lead me.

Father, guard the walls of my heart. Lord, cultivate the soil of my heart with Your Word. Lord, let Your Wisdom flourish in every aspect of my life. Father, guide the course of my destiny. Lord, lead my pathway.

Father, let not my heart be entangled in the bondage of the past. Father, remove the chains of the past. Lord, lead me and I will be made whole. Lord, guide me and I will be set free. Lord, wash me and I will be made whiter than snow. Father, guide my tongue. Lord, lead my heart. Father, guide the work of my hands. Lord, guide my day. Father, I surrender to You, now and forever.

In Jesus' Name. Amen.

FOR MORE BOOKS VISIT
www.VanceKJackson.com

www.ingramcontent.com/pod-product-compliance
Lightning Source LLC
Chambersburg PA
CBHW030914080526
44589CB00010B/293